Sense of Self

A Coping and Life Skills Workbook For Teens and Adults

by Sally Safadi
Copyright © 2020 Neurons Away

SENSE OF SELF
Distress Tolerance Skills Packet

Written and Created by Sally Safadi

Published by Neurons Away LLC
Syracuse, New York
Copyright © 2020 Neurons Away

ALL RIGHTS RESERVED WORLDWIDE.
No part of this publication may be reproduced in any material form (including photocopying of any pages other than the illustrated handouts, storing it in any medium by electronic means and whether or not transiently or incidentally to some other use of this publication) without the written permission of the copyright owner. Applications for the copyright owner's written permission to reproduce any part of this publication should be addressed to the publisher.

NOT FOR COMMERCIAL USE.

Permission must be granted in written form by Neurons Away

Hello there,

This vibrant series focuses on the effectiveness and success of various coping and life skills. The workbook includes easy to read instructions, questions and activities that draw from DBT, CBT, educational theories and self-care practices.

Handouts are visually appealing and interactive worksheets are available to increase the effectiveness and success of the various stress tolerance techniques.

These worksheets are only intended as supplemental tools to your practice and do not need to be done in any specific order. Just pick and choose whatever you'd like to work on.

You may use the material for one on one or small group sessions. If you wish to use make large number of photocopes for big groups or for commerical use please contact neuronsaway@gmail.com.

Large sized posters that can be used in waiting rooms or therapy spaces can be purchased at **neuronsaway.com**

Thank you very much for your support! If you have any suggestions or would like to see a new coping skill added to the collection please reach out.

Have a great day!

5. Breathing
6. Breathing Worksheet
7. Belly Breathing
8. Butterfly Hug
9. Butterfly Worksheet
10. Meditation
11. Meditation Worksheet
12. Self-Awareness
13. Building You Character
14. Character Worksheet
15. Reflection Worksheet
16. Healthy Socializing
17. 5 People Worksheet
18. Conversation Starters
19. Activities
20. 5-4-3-2-1 Relax
21. 5-4-3-2-1 Worksheet
22. Your Self-Talk
23. Self-Talk Worksheet
24. Use Your Hands
25. Use Your Hand Worksheet
26. Wash Hands
27. Movement is Medicine
28. Movement Worksheet
29. Movement is medicine (seated)
30. Seated Worksheet
31. Mindful Walking
32. Walking Worksheet
33. Mindful Walking worksheet
34. Understanding Your Story
35. Transform your story
36. List all possibilities worksheet
37. Story about yourself worksheet
38. Create Your Life worksheet
39. Acts of self-care
40. Importance of selfcare worksheet
41. Healthy distractions
42. Vision Board
43. Blessings bowl
44. Create a plant
45. Connect Constellation

{Breathing}

Breathing is the process of inhaling and exhaling air from the lungs. When a person inhales, the lungs expand and pull life-sustaining oxygen into the body. When a person exhales, the lungs contract, and a waste product called carbon dioxide is pushed out of the body.

Breathing is simple, free, and with you at all times.

Easy Deep Breathing Exercise

1. **Inhale through the nose for 3 counts**
   (while breathing in count 1..2..3..)

2. **Hold your breath for 3 counts**
   (while holding your breath count 1..2..3..)

3. **Exhale through your mouth for 3 counts**
   (while breathing out count 1..2..3...)

*Repeat for 5 minutes

The benefits of deep breathing.
- *Relieves pain and emotional distress*
- *Improves your sleep and eating cycles*
- *Relaxes the mind and brings clarity*
- *Improves your mood and mindset*

"A healthy mind has an easy breath."

Breathing is one of the greatest pleasures in life.

Easy Deep Breathing Activity

1. Inhale through the nose for 3 counts
(while breathing in count 1..2..3..)

what do you want to bring in?

2. Hold your breath for 3 counts
(while holding your breath count 1..2..3...)

what do you want to hold within you?

3. Exhale through your mouth for 3 counts
(while breathing out count 1..2..3...)

why is breathing so important?

what do you want to release?

Belly Breathing

Also known as diaphragmatic breathing or abdominal breathing.

It gets its name from the way you use the diaphragm
(which sits below the lungs) to fully saturate the lungs with oxygen.
This has the effect of pushing the belly outward.

Step 1: Sit or Lie Comfortably

Find a comfortable, quiet place to sit or lie down.

If in a chair, sit up with and your neck and shoulders relaxed and your knees bent.

If you're lying down, you can place a pillow under your head and knees.

Step 2: Arrange Your Hands

Place one hand on your upper chest over you heart.

The other hand should be just above your belly button.
You should be able to feel your diaphragm go up and down.

Step 3: Breathe In Through Your Nose

The air going in through your nose should push your abdominal muscles outward so that you can feel your stomach rise with your lower hand.

Air flow should be smooth and the top hand should remain still.

Step 4: Breathe Out Through Your Mouth

Purse your lips and exhale slowly.

Let your stomach area relax. You should feel the hand that's over it fall inward (toward your spine). Don't squeeze your stomach, let it fall naturally.

The hand on your chest should continue to remain still.

© 2020 Neurons Away

Butterfly Hug

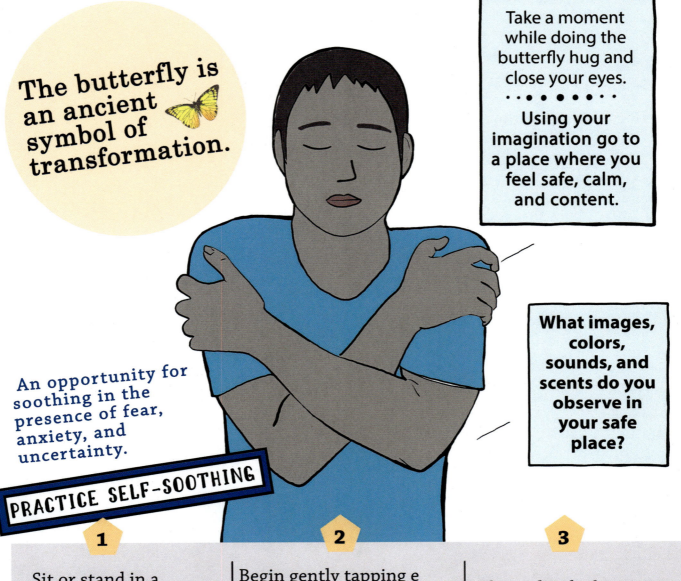

The butterfly is an ancient symbol of transformation.

Take a moment while doing the butterfly hug and close your eyes.
. . . .
Using your imagination go to a place where you feel safe, calm, and content.

An opportunity for soothing in the presence of fear, anxiety, and uncertainty.

What images, colors, sounds, and scents do you observe in your safe place?

PRACTICE SELF-SOOTHING

1
Sit or stand in a comfortable position.

Cross both arms in front of your chest and place each hand on your upper arms.

2
Begin gently tapping each hand one at a time on your arms.

Practice relaxed breathing. You may be surprised to discover you are feeling calmer.

3
If your level of anxiety or anger doesn't change at all, give yourself some more time with the butterfly hug and see what happens.

Butterfly Hug

BENEFITS OF BUTTERFLY HUG
- Self-soothing and calming
- Promotes emotion regulation
- Comforting and relaxing
- Promotes self-compassion

Draw a place where you feel safe, calm, and content.

What colors, sounds, and scents do you observe in your safe place?

Create a cool butterfly.

Take a moment while doing the butterfly hug and close your eyes.

Name _____ Date ___/___/___

Meditation

Benefits:
- Speeds up recovery
- Improves decision-making skills
- Enhances focus and concentration
- Reduces panic and stress

Meditation is like taking a multivitamin for your health. It is great to do it every day.

1. Use your inner voice to prepare for meditation by repeating helpful sentences such as:
- "I am creating a safe space."
- "Every day in every way, I'm getting better and better."
- "I am happy, healthy and whole."
- "I am safe and sound. All is well."

2. Get in a comfortable position in a quiet space.
Examples:
- Sit up right in a chair
- Lay down on a bed
- Sit cross-legged on the ground

3. FOCUS ON YOUR BREATH
- Feel the air enter your nose
- Feel your lungs fill up with air
- Feel the air leaving your nose or mouth.

Start with 4 breaths work your way up to more.

4. Close your eyes and clear your mind
- Smile softly, feel it.
- Listen to your natural breathing
- Observe your heartbeat

TIPS:
- Listen to calming music or a guided meditation
- Softly hum a tune or repeat a mantra
- Write in a journal before and after meditating
- Create a space with items or pictures you admire.

© 2020 Neurons Away

Meditation

How do you think meditation will help you?

Benefits:
-
-
-
-

Meditation is like taking a multivitamin for your health. It is great to do it every day.

1. Write your Mantra.
A mantra is usually a phrase or sentence repeated in meditation.

2. Where and how do you feel most comfortable meditating?

3. How can conscious breathing help you?

4. What does it mean to clear your mind?

Circle the ones you'd like to practice with your meditation:
- ★ Listen to calming music or a guided meditation
- ★ Softly hum a tune or repeat a mantra
- ★ Write in a journal before and after meditating
- ★ Create a space with items or pictures you admire.

Name _____ Date ___/___/_____   © 2020 Neurons Away   11

Self Awareness

Self-awareness is simply being aware of who you are, what you're like, and what you're capable of.

What is Self-Awareness?

Self-awareness is having a clear understanding of your personality and behavior. This includes your strengths, weaknesses, beliefs, motivations, and emotions.

"To know thyself is the beginning of wisdom."

Why practicing self-awareness is important:

→ You will have **better self-control** over your behavior and **respond better** to outside interactions.

→ You will **be aware of your true goals** and values allowing for better decision making.

→ You can **build a better foundation for yourself to grow** from, rather than being influenced by unhealthy people.

You will have more inner peace and be happier in expressing your true-self.

How to develop self-awareness

- **Frequently ask yourself the right questions.** What inspires you? What are your goals this year?

- **Think about how your day went.** Did you overreact to anything? What did you handle well?

- **Relax and meditate.** Give yourself space and time to let your thoughts and emotions flow naturally.

Strengthening your sense of self.

"The way that we perceive ourselves is the way that we present ourselves".

Life can be challenging and full of surprises. Without a strong and developed sense of awareness it's easy to become overwhelmed and lose focus. Try some of the suggestions below to build awareness and strengthen your character.

→ **Change the words or phrases you use.**
The way you communicate represents you. If you want to be more positive you must use encouraging and helpful words.

→ **Surround yourself with positive influences.**
It's important to choose people, videos, talks, books, etc. that reflect and inspire the choices you desire to make in life.

→ **Change up your style, clothes or accessories.**
Dress the mood you want to feel. If you want to feel more confident dress in something that reflects confidence.

→ **Read fiction.**
Reading fiction allows you to learn about different personalities and traits that you could reflect in your own character.

→ **Try new activities.**
Trying new activities is a great way to learn what you are capable of and allows you to build on a variety of skills.

→ **Write a letter to yourself**
What do you have to say to yourself? Simply getting your thoughts on a piece of paper can be a good way to self-reflect.

→ **Incorporate exercise into your daily habits.**
Exercise and regular body movement are some of the best ways to improve your self-percpetion and boost your energy.

Name _____ Date ____/____/_____   © 2020 Neurons Away

Do you see yourself for who you really are?

Understand yourself by asking the right questions

What's most important to you?

What makes you happy?

What influences your behavior?

What are your strengths?

What are weaknesses you want to improve upon?

How can you get to know yourself more?

What do you see in your reflection?

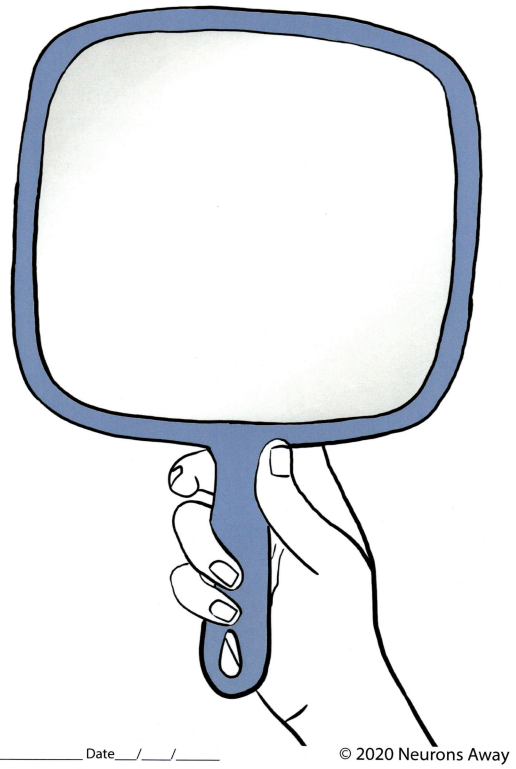

Healthy Socializing

Socializing means interacting with various people, groups and communities.

- Meeting new people
- Establishing friendships
- Enjoying the company of others
- Connecting with others
- Joining community activities

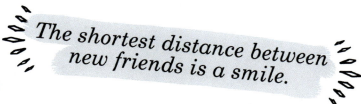
The shortest distance between new friends is a smile.

Why is healthy socializing important?

Social interactions have a positive influence on one's physical, mental & spiritual health.

→ Helps form a variety of meaningful and growth promoting relationships

→ Builds self-confidence and improves communication skills

→ Can gain a better understanding of available opportunities.

Ways to build healthy social connections:

Positive & creative interactions help improve your environment.

- Introduce yourself to someone new
- Take a walk with a friend
- Play a game or read with others
- Teach someone a skill you may have
- Ask someone to teach you a skill
- Join an activity group
- Make something together
- Help out someone in need
- Ask someone to be your exercising buddy
- Write a poem with someone

The ❺ people you spend the most time with help shape who you are.

We are greatly influenced by the relationships closest to us. It affects our way of thinking, our self-esteem, and our decisions. Of course, everyone is their own person, but sometimes we are affected by our environment in more ways that we may understand.

1.
List 5 ways you could improve your current relationships/friendships.
_____
_____
_____
_____
_____

2.
List 5 different groups, activities or communities you are intersted in joining.
_____
_____
_____
_____
_____

3.
List 5 characteristics you are looking for in a new friend.
_____
_____
_____
_____
_____

4.
List 5 ways you can re-direct an unhealthy social environment.
_____
_____
_____
_____
_____

5. **List 5 traits you want to gain from your social interactions.**

Conversation Starters:

Sitting with some friends or a new group of people?
Try sparking a conversation with one of the questions below:

Group Game
1. Begin by letting one person choose a question.
2. Going in a circle, let each person respond.
   (the person who chose the questions goes last)
3. Each player must provide a response within a total time of 3 minutes.
   (3 minutes for the entire group NOT each person)
4. If the group goes over 3 minutes the person who chose the question gets to make a rule.
   (example: raise both arms while talking)
5. For each round completed within 3 mins the group gets 5 points. (adjust time if necessary)

1. What is your favorite food?
2. What's your favorite season? Why?
3. Where do good thoughts and ideas come from?
4. What would it feel like to be a tree?
5. What are three things you want to learn?
6. Where is the most beautiful place near where you live?
7. What do you do to improve your mood when you are in a bad mood?
8. What do you have that you are grateful for?
9. What would life be like if there was no such thing as sound?
10. What are the good things in life?
11. Where does wisdom come from?
12. Where does happiness come from?
13. What are three things the world needs more of?
14. What's the coolest thing you've ever seen?
15. What makes up a good community?
16. What are some of your favorite movies?

Add some new questions to the list.

Name_____ Date___/___/_____ © 2020 Neurons Away

Circle the activities you would like to try and place a star next your top three choices.

To lead a fulfilling and happy life it is important to stay engaged and active in the community. Joining new classes, involving yourself in new activities and staying physically active can change and improve the dynamics of your lifestyle.

Things to do just for fun
1. Kite Flying
2. Trip to the Museum
3. Visit a second-hand shop
4. Trip to an Art Gallery
5. Attend a theatre show
6. Trip to an amusement park
7. Attend a concert
8. Visit a zoo or animal shelter
9. Spend the day at the beach
10. Go see a movie
11. Volunteer
12. Read
13. Write a short book
14. Take day trip
15. Skip rocks
16. Sudoku
17. Crossword puzzles
18. Word searches
19. Chess
20. Checkers
21. Scrabble
22. Card games
23. Create card pyramids
24. Dominoes
25. Bingo
26. Learn to meditate
27. Nature walk/hike
28. Visit a café
29. Part time job/volunteer
30. Explore your city

Team Sports
31. Hockey
32. Soccer
33. Basketball
34. Baseball
35. Football
36. Volleyball
37. Rugby
38. Ultimate Frisbee
39. Lacrosse
40. Tennis
41. Bowling
42. Fencing
43. Golf
44. Synchronized swimming

Sports/Activities
45. Swimming
46. Running/Jogging
47. Kayaking
48. Martial Arts
49. Biking
50. Canoeing
51. Rock Climbing
52. Snowboarding
53. Skiing
54. Surfing
55. Skating
56. Roller blading
57. Calisthenics
58. Archery
59. Fishing
60. Gymnastics
61. Yoga
62. Acrobatics
63. Pilates
64. Tai Chi
65. Hiking
66. Horseback riding
67. Juggling
68. Scuba diving
69. Snorkeling
70. Weight lifting
71. Tread mill

Dance
72. Irish dancing
73. Salsa dancing
74. Hip hop
75. Tap
76. Swing
77. Belly-dancing
78. Ballet
79. Break-dancing
80. Zumba

Creative Hobbies
81. Cooking/Baking
82. Cake Making / Decorating
83. Sculpting
84. Furniture building
85. Woodcarving
86. Flower arranging
87. Coloring
88. Watercolor painting
89. Oil painting
90. Glass painting
91. Chalk drawing
92. Rapping/Free styling
93. Collecting (e.g. stamps)
94. Origami
95. Calligraphy
96. Jewelry making
97. Gardening
98. Magic tricks
99. Photography
100. Writing
101. Poetry writing
102. Sewing
103. Knitting
104. Embroidery
105. Making dream-catchers
106. Weaving (baskets, etc)
107. Scrap-booking
108. Learn to play a musical instrument. (guitar, flute)
109. Learn a new language
110. Restoration/refurbishing
111. Canning/jarring

5-4-3-2-1-Relax

Engage your 5 senses to help you reconnect and feel calmer in the present moment.

SIGHT — Observe your surroundings

Identify 5 of each:
- circular objects
- rectangular objects
- items that are blue
- items that can fit in your hand

TOUCH — Feel with your hands

Find & feel 4 items for 20 seconds each
1. a hard and sturdy item
2. a soft or fluffy item
3. a flexible and bendy item
4. a rough or bumpy item

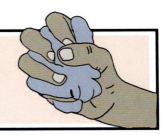

HEARING — Listen to your surroundings

Identify 3 different sounds
1. listen to the sounds close to you
2. listen for background sounds
3. listen to sound of your breath

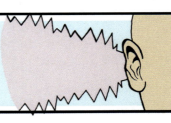

SMELL — Engage your nose

Sniff out 2 scents from your surrounding
1. a scent that you enjoy (flowers, soap, bread, etc.)
2. a strong scent that stimulates your nose (coffee, lotion, etc.)

TASTE — On the tip of your tongue

Engage your taste buds by trying 1 of each: Something **Sweet,** something **Sour** and something **Salty.**

Name _____ Date ___/___/_____   © 2020 Neurons Away

5-4-3-2-1-Relax
Engage your 5 senses to help you reconnect and feel calmer in the present moment.

5 **Observe your surroundings and identify 5 of the following:**

Circular objects	Rectangular objects	Blue items	Items that can fit in your hand
_____	_____	_____	_____
_____	_____	_____	_____
_____	_____	_____	_____
_____	_____	_____	_____
_____	_____	_____	_____

4 **Find and feel 4 items** - *touch or hold for 10 seconds each*

a hard item   a soft item   a flexible item   a smooth item

_____   _____   _____   _____

3 **Listen to your surroundings and identify 3 different sounds:**

[_____]   [_____]   [_____]

2 **Engage your nose by sniffing out 2 different smells**
Seek out scents you enjoy such as flowers, coffee, lotion etc.

[_____]   [_____]

1 **On the tip of your tongue try tasting one of the following**
OR find and try them all! *(If you don't have access to food at the moment use your imagination. Imagine biting into a lemon or sprinkling salt on your tongue.)*

     Sweet   **Sour**   and **Salty**

Name _____ Date ___/___/_____

The Art of Self Talk

What is self-talk? It's the voice in your head that narrates your life and perspective. Sometimes it can have a negative or positive impact on your emotions.

1 Monitor your self-talk
Listen to what you're saying to yourself.

Spend a few days listening to your inner dialogue.
- Are you aware of what you are saying to yourself?
- Where are these thoughts and words coming from?
- Are they words you picked up from others?

2 Identify Your Tone
Is your self-talk helpful or non-helpful?

Take sometime to learn and understand your self-talk.
- Is your inner dialogue making you feel better or worse?
- Would you be comfortable saying those thoughts and words to a loved one?

3 Improve your self-talk
How can you adjust your self-talk to better suit you?

Make an effort to choose words and phrases that make you feel better.
- What can you say to yourself to boost your confidence?
- What words can you use to improve your mood or calm you down?

© 2020 Neurons Away

The Art of Self Talk

Use this worksheet to learn more about your inner dialogue

What is self-talk? It's the voice in your head that narrates your life and perspective. Sometimes it can have a negative or positive impact on your emotions.

If in a group setting:
- Discuss where different kinds of self-talk come from.
- How it can affect your mindset and well-being.
- Share examples of healthy self-talk.

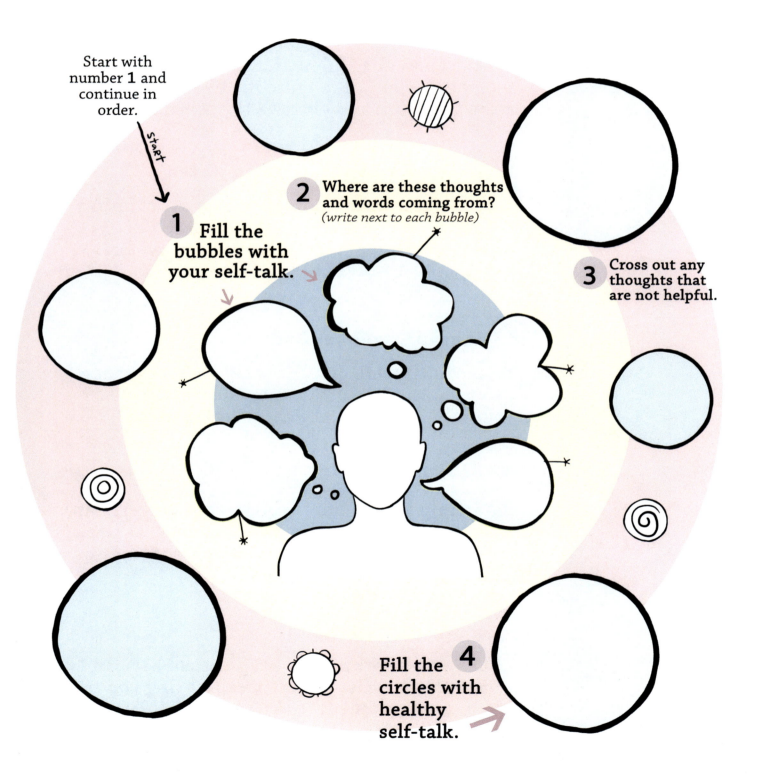

Start with number 1 and continue in order.

1 Fill the bubbles with your self-talk.

2 Where are these thoughts and words coming from? *(write next to each bubble)*

3 Cross out any thoughts that are not helpful.

4 Fill the circles with healthy self-talk.

Name _____ Date ___/___/_____

© 2020 Neurons Away

USE YOUR HANDS
to redirect or distract thoughts when dealing with a difficult situation.

> Often the hands will solve a mystery that the intellect has struggled with in vain.
> -Carl Jung

START SMALL & SIMPLE

Boost Resilience

1- Hold an ice cube
Find an ice cube and hold it in your hand for as long as you can tolerate it. Give the ice cube attention and observe the sensation.

Ease Anxiety

2- Wash your hands in warm water
Warm water immediately engages a calming response. In the moment of a stressful event, removing yourself to wash your hands can give you both the space and body connection to regain composure.

De-stress

3 - Squeeze a rubber ball
Squeeze the ball for a few seconds and then release. As your muscles relax, the tension will leave your arms and hands, thereby relieving stress.

Learn adaptability

4 - Squish playdough
Squishing playdough through your fingers can release aggression, frustration, anger. As tension is relieved use the play dough to create shapes and express your creativity.

Redirect Concentration

5- Snap a rubber band
When you have anxiety, snap the rubber band against your wrist a few times to bring you to the present moment. Take this moment to choose a new thought or say something calming to yourself.

USE YOUR HANDS

Using a stress ball can help redirect your mind away from stress and help you to relax

Design this stress ball →

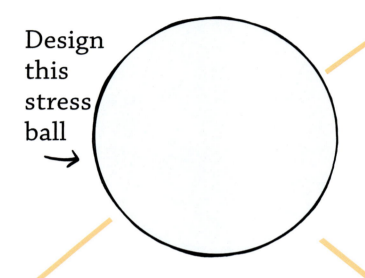

Squeeze a rubber ball

1. Hold the ball in your hand notice the weight and texture.
2. Squeeze the ball as tight as possible for 5 seconds.
3. Release your grip for 5 seconds
4. Repeat 10 times.

When you are experiencing high stress or overwhelming emotions, your body is holding a lot of unhealthy energy and it has no where to go.
A physical release is a helpful way to let go of that unhealthy energy.

Place all your **feelings** in this ball.
(write or draw)

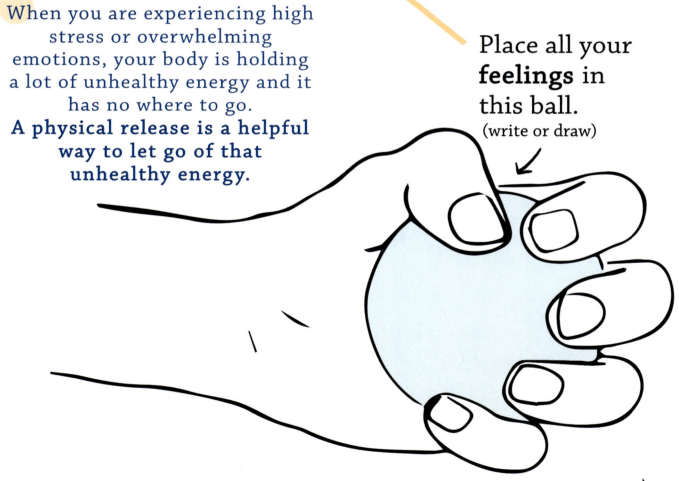

Wash your hands in warm water

Warm water immediately engages a calming response.
In the moment of a stressful event, removing yourself to wash your hands can give you both the space and body connection to regain composure.

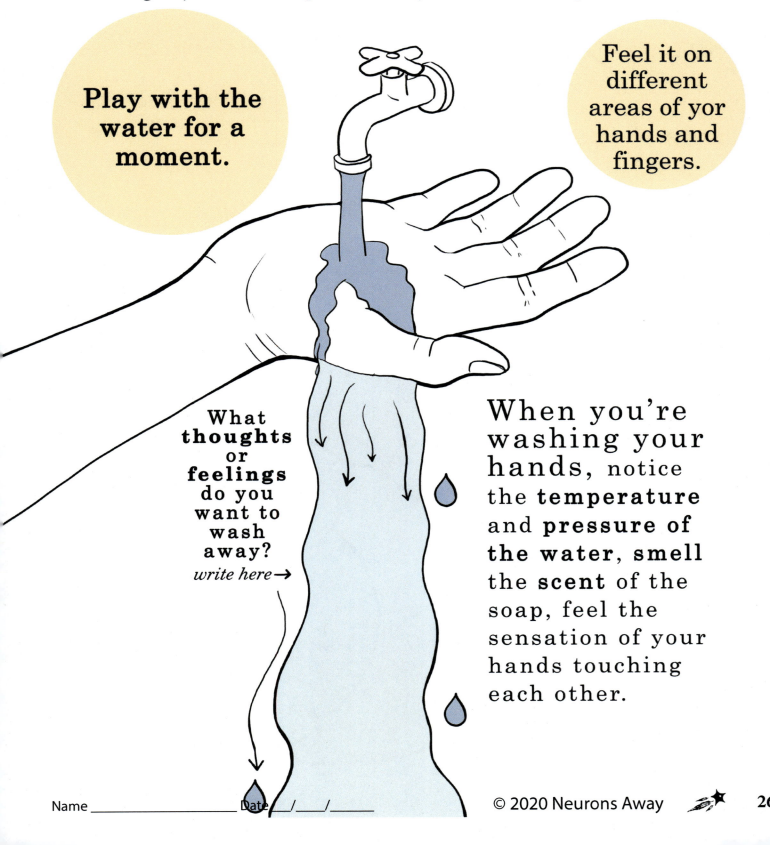

Play with the water for a moment.

Feel it on different areas of yor hands and fingers.

What **thoughts or feelings** do you want to wash away?
write here →

When you're washing your hands, notice the **temperature** and **pressure of the water**, smell the **scent** of the soap, feel the sensation of your hands touching each other.

© 2020 Neurons Away

Movement is Medicine

Moving the body can create change in a person's physical, emotional, and mental states.

Exercising your core improves strength, balance, coordination and flexibility.

Do 10 sit ups **or** Kick your feet like you are riding a bicycle for 1 minute

Touch your toes for 1 minute **or** Reach for the sky then touch your toes 20 times

Hold a plank for 30 seconds 2 times **or** Attempt to do 5 pushups 2 times.

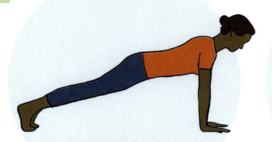

Moving the whole body is an energising and effective way to relieve stress and anxiety

Dance for 2 or more minutes **or** Run in place for 1 minute

Do 20 jumping jacks 2 times **or** Hold your hands high in the air for 1 minute

Kick each leg up 10 times **or** Bring your knee up to your opposite elbow 10 times each side

Name_____ Date___/___/_____   © 2020 Neurons Away

Movement is Medicine
Moving the body can create change in a person's physical, emotional, and mental states.

COLOR AND PLAY
1. Choose an exercise from the page to do.
2. After you perform the exercises color in the figure you chose
3. Contiune until all figures are colored in.

IF PLAYING IN A GROUP
1. Choose an exercise (a or b) for everyone in the group to complete.
2. Color the figure in after the exercises has been completed.
3. Contiune until all figures are fully colored in.
(for an extra challenge complete both a & b exercises)

2 a - Dance for 1 one minute
or b - Run in place for 1 minute

1 a - Do 20 jumping jacks
or b - Hold your hands high in the air for 1

3 a - Kick each leg up 10 times
or b - Bring your knee up to your opposite elbow 10 times each side

4 a - Hold a plank for 30 seconds
or b - Attempt to do 5 pushups

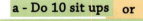

a - Do 10 sit ups   or
b - Kick your feet like you are riding a bicycle for 1 minute

5

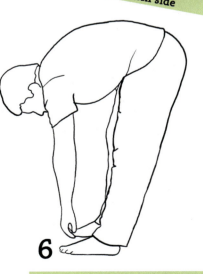

6 a - Touch your toes for 1 minute
or b - Reach for the sky then touch your toes 20 times

Name _____ Date ___/___/_____   © 2020 Neurons Away   28

Movement is Medicine

Moving Your Body Is Good for Your Mind
Exercise releases endorphins, which create feelings of happiness and helps boost self-esteem and confidence.

Seated Jacks
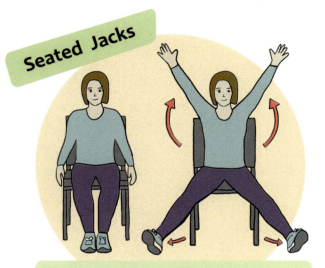

1. Start at the edge of your seat, knees bent and arms at your side.
2. Then at the same time raise your arms and extend your legs wide to the sides Bring arms and legs back to center.
3. Repeat 20 times.

Seated Twists
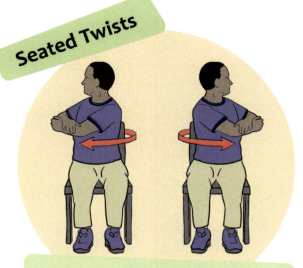

1. Fold your arms in front of you.
2. Turn your upper body to the side let your head follow last.

   Twist to the other side.
3. Go slow and repeat this 20 times.

Leg Extensions

1. Hold the side of your chair for support. Lift and extend one leg in front of you.
2. Then lift the other leg. Repeat on each side 10 times.

Peekaboo

1. Hold your arms up to the side with elbows bent and palms facing forward.
2. Bring your forearms together in front of your face. Repeat 20 times.

© 2020 Neurons Away

Movement is Medicine (Seated Exercises)

Various forms of exercises can boost your mood, ease depression and anxiety enhance your self-esteem, and improve your whole outlook on life.

COLOR AND PLAY
1. Choose an exercise from the page to do.
2. After you perform the exercises color in the figure you chose
3. Contiune until all figures are colored in.

IF PLAYING IN A GROUP
1. Choose an exercise for everyone in the group to complete.
2. Color the figure in after the exercises has been completed.
3. Contiune until all figures are fully colored in.

Seated Twists 3
Twist your upper body from side to side. Repeat 10 times on each side.

March in Place 2
While seated march in place. Swing the opposite arm as you march each foot forward.

Peekaboo 4
Bring your forearms together in front of your face. Repeat 20 times.

1 **Seated Jacks**
Raise your arms and extend your legs wide and to the sides. Repeat 20 times.

5 **Arm Extensions**
Stretch and reach each arm high over your head. Repeat 20 times.

6 **Leg Extensions**
Lift and extend each leg up. Repeat on each leg 10 times.

7 **Leg Extensions**
Extend your arms to the side. Rotate shoulders and arms 20 times forward and 20 times backwards.

Name_____ Date___/___/_____   © 2020 Neurons Away

Mindful Walking

A great way to regulate emotions, calm the body, and focus the mind.

UNWIND YOUR MIND

1

Find a clear space where you can walk about 10 feet or more.

Bring your awareness down to your feet. **Shift your weight from side to side and tap each foot gently against the floor.**

2

Take a deep breath, lift your head and look straight ahead with your chest held high.

Place your hands to your side or hold them behind your back.

Begin walking, extend one foot and feel it touch the ground.

As you step forward notice how the other leg begins to lift up.

3

Continue walking forward. On your tenth step stop and take a deep breath.

Turn around and walk back to the other side continuing the same practice.

Do this for about 10 to 15 minutes or until you are feeling better.

Callouts on figure:
- Notice how your body feels. Does it feel heavy or light, stiff or relaxed?
- When your mind wanders refocus on your feet and body movement.
- Notice the motions and position of your arms and hands as you walk.
- Feel the muscles from your hips to your feet as they tighten and relax.
- Let anything that makes you feel angry or anxious be released from your feet into the ground.

Name _____ Date ___/___/_____ © 2020 Neurons Away

Mindful Walking

A great way to regulate emotions, calm the body, and focus the mind.

Find a clear space where you can walk about 10 feet or more.

Bring your awareness down to your feet. **Shift your weight from side to side and tap each foot gently against the floor.**

Take a deep breath, lift your head and look straight ahead with your chest held high.

Place your hands to your side or hold them behind your back.

Begin walking, extend one foot and feel it touch the ground.

As you step forward notice how the other leg begins to lift up.

Continue walking forward. On your tenth step stop and **take a deep breath.**

Turn around and walk back to the other side continuing the same practice.

Do this for about 10 to 15 minutes or until you are feeling better.

Before Walking:

How are you currently feeling?
(Write down at least three emotions)

_____
_____
_____

Circle where you feel these emotions:
(if they are emotions you wish to release, draw lines that release them through the feet)

How and **why** might mindful walking help you release unwanted feelings?

_____
_____
_____

After Walking:

How are you currently feeling?
(Write down at least three emotions)

_____
_____
_____

Draw one thing you remember from your walk:

Do you feel a difference?

Yes / No

If yes explain why:

_____
_____
_____

If no explain why and what you might do differently next time:

_____
_____
_____
_____
_____

Name _____ Date ___/___/_____

© 2020 Neurons Away

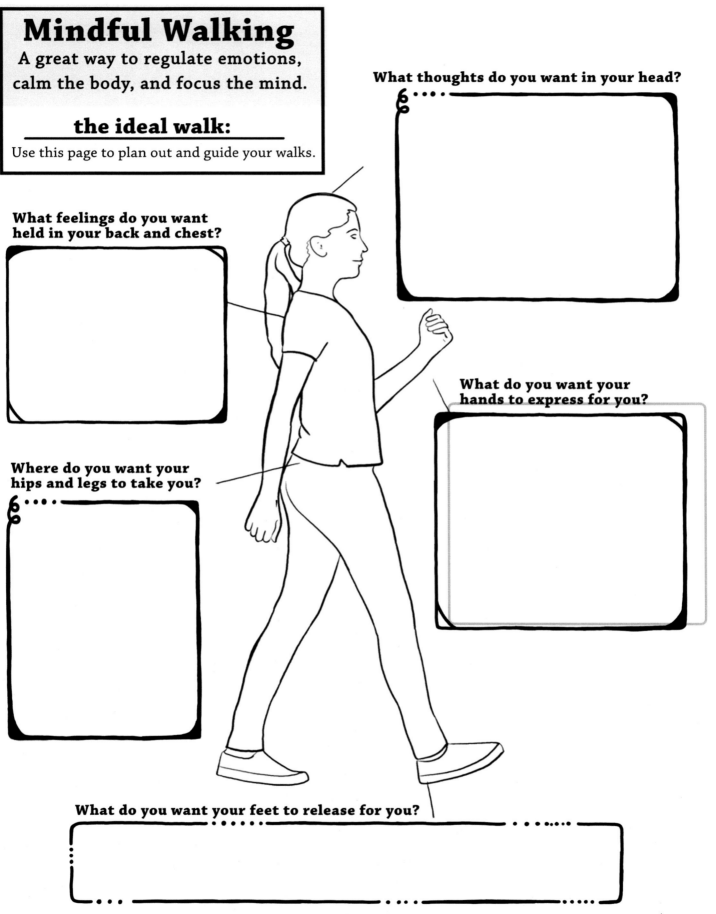

Shifting Your Story

Let go of the past, feel content in the present, and create a fulfilling future.

 What's your story?

 A story is the narrative you identify yourself by. It's how you introduce yourself and interact with the world. Your story influences your perspective and decisions making.

 How do these stories form?

 The stories we live by are influenced by our **past experiences**, by the **words and actions others convey to us** and by our **ingrained beliefs**. These influences can be negative, positive or neutral.

 Identify what's helping and what's hindering.

 It's important to understand the stories and beliefs you hold close to you. Are they **mental blocks or growth promoting thoughts**? Does a past mistake still hold you back now?

 Transforming the stories.

 You might not be able to control the facts of your life, but **you can control your interpretation.** You have the ability to revise beliefs and thoughts. You have the ability to tell new stories.

Transform your story

Your past doesn't dictate your future.

 Remember the past is the past and the time now is an opportunity to make new and better choices despite what has happened before. By repeating past stories over and over again we bring them into the present which can limit future choices.

6 ways to revise your story:

Purpose:
New outlook on life
Creating change from within
Opens up new opportunities

Use your imagination creatively.
When you imagine yourself succeeding at something you can generate a sense of confidence or excitement. But if for example you choose to engage your imagination by worrying that produces anxiety and stress.

Visualize yourself doing something different
Imagine yourself doing something complete different, like climbing up a mountain, swimming in the ocean, walking through a rain forest. What sounds do you hear, what scents do you smell, what colors do you hear?

List all the different possibilities
Take a moment and think about all the possible outcomes you have for yourself. Write them down even if some are out of your comfort zone.
List all possible scenarios, jobs, studies, hobbies etc.

Use helpful self-talk
Developing an encouraging day to day internal script, helps transform your long-term stories. If you normally start the day by saying "I'm not a morning person." instead try saying, "I'm learning to embrace the whole day."

Write an inspiring story about yourself
You can use experiences from the past or dive deep into your imagination. Either way write a story that lifts your spirits and makes you smile.
"I won the lottery and it's been great!" or "I finally opened my cupcake shop!"

Add play to your life.
Playing with partners, friends, co-workers, pets, and children is a great way to improve problem-solving abilities and enhance emotional well-being.
You'll see situations in life as opportunities to advance rather than dead-ends.

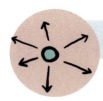 # List all the different possibilities

Take a moment and think about all the possible outcomes you have for yourself. Write them down even if some are out of your comfort zone. List all possible senarios, jobs, studies, hobbies, etc. (Add more arrows if you need to.)

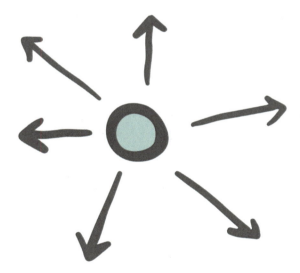

Write an inspiring story about yourself

You can use experiences from the past or dive deep into your imagination. Either way write a story that lifts your spirits and makes you smile. "I invented a cool new toy!" or "I finally got to see my favorite animal up close!"

Re-Imagine Yourself

Re-imagining is the continuous activity of reflection and choice. It involves rearranging and understanding our priorities in life and rediscovering a new sense of being alive.

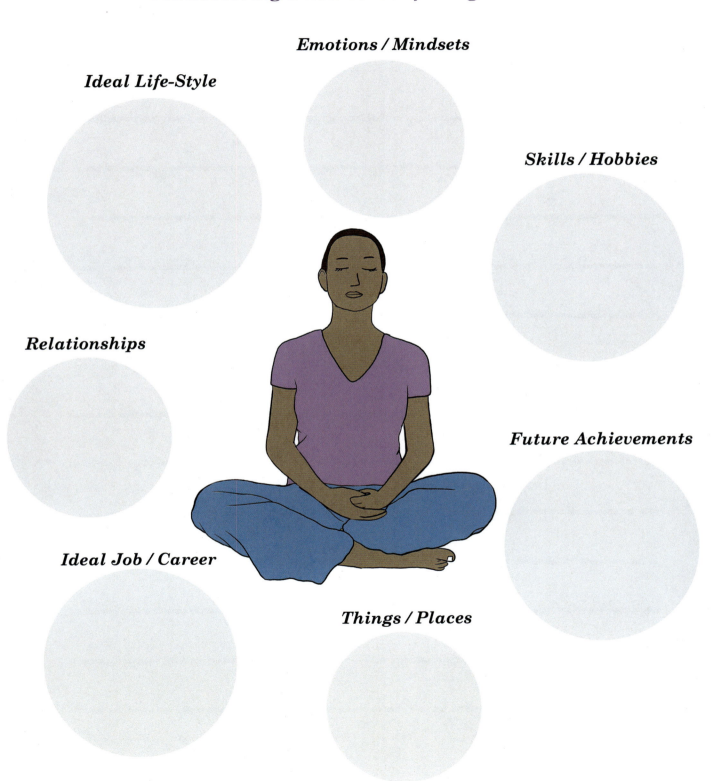

Acts of Self Care

Self-care is the active participation in enhancing your quality of life. This includes emotional, physical and spiritual wellbeing

CHOOSE 3 OF YOUR FAVORITE ACTIVITIES TO DO TODAY

- write in a journal
- take a hot shower
- read a book /fiction
- sing or listen to music
- write a song or poetry
- drink a cup of hot tea
- drink lots of water
- write a nice letter to yourself
- create a vision board
- engage in positive self-talk
- create a new schedule for yourself
- learn a healthy recipe
- list everything you are proud of
- meditate or do yoga
- call a close friend for a chat
- massage your head and neck
- rub lotion on your hands
- Take deep breaths
- Brush your teeth
- Smile

It is important to give yourself time and space to include self-beneficial activities throughout your week.

"The way you treat yourself sets the standard for others."

The Importance of Self Care

Self-care is the active participation in enhancing your quality of life. This includes emotional, physical and spiritual wellbeing

List the ways you can care for yourself

It is important to give yourself time and space to include self-beneficial activities throughout your week.

"The way you treat yourself sets the standard for others."

Distract Yourself in Healthy Ways

Perhaps the simplest way to calm your mind is to distract yourself by focusing on some other thought, interest, or activity that holds and redirects your attention.

CHOOSE 3 TO DO TODAY

- ☐ Learn to juggle
- ☐ Doodle or draw
- ☐ Plan a journey
- ☐ Listen to music
- ☐ Floss your teeth
- ☐ Eat a piece of fruit
- ☐ Learn to moonwalk
- ☐ Daydream
- ☐ Squeeze your pillow
- ☐ Take a nap
- ☐ Memorize a poem
- ☐ Learn origami
- ☐ Draw a self portrait
- ☐ Write a bucket list
- ☐ Play solitaire
- ☐ Make up some jokes
- ☐ Draw your favorite room
- ☐ Leave nice notes in random places
- ☐ Learn about a new culture
- ☐ Celebrate a small success
- ☐ Make up a new smoothie recipe
- ☐ Write a list of fun things to do
- ☐ Learn or make up a new song
- ☐ Clean/reorganize your space
- ☐ Give yourself a foot massage
- ☐ Write a letter to a friend
- ☐ Watch a new movie or TV show
- ☐ Share a funny story
- ☐ Draw the cover to your book
- ☐ Write a list of your achievements

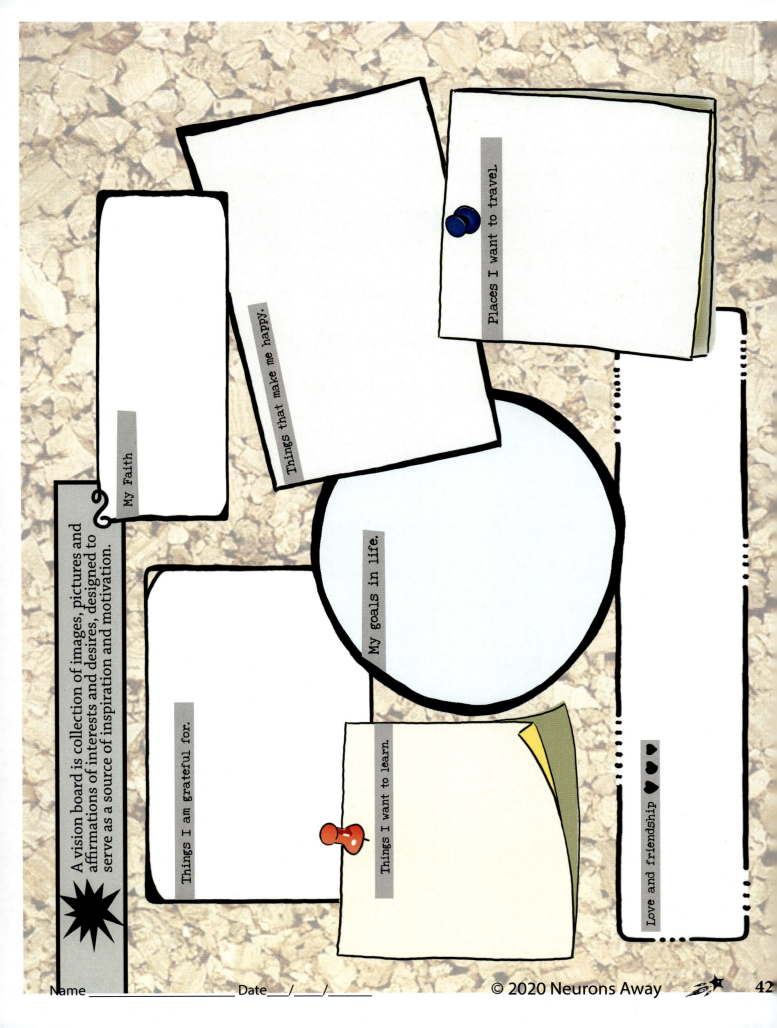

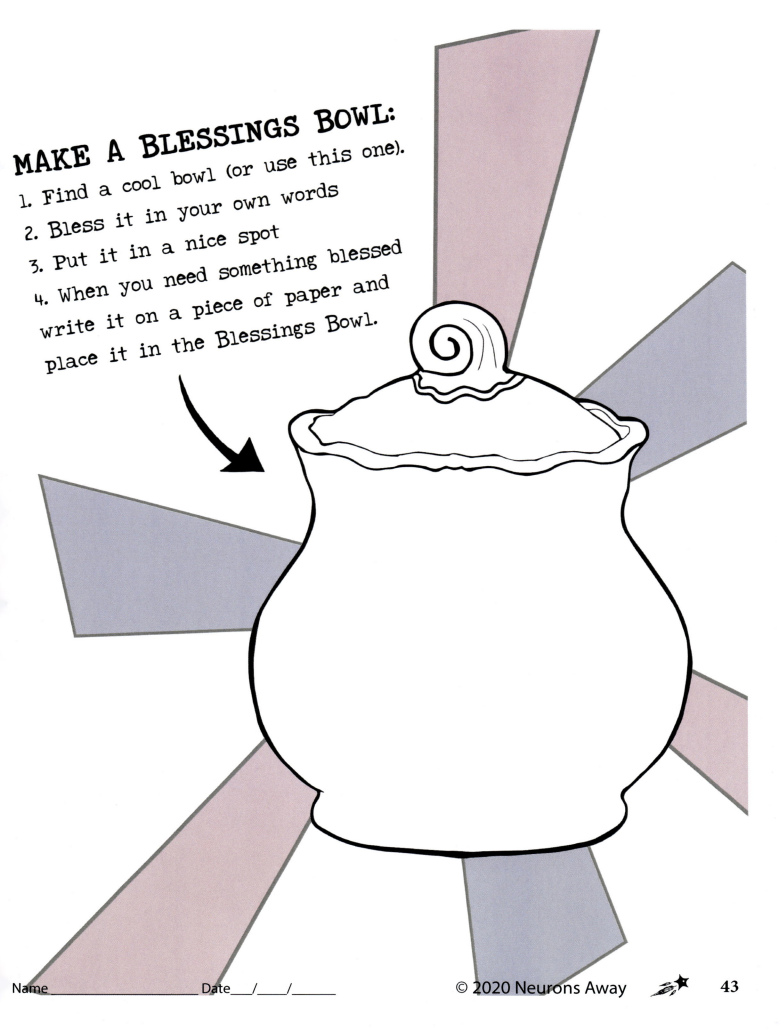

Create a new plant

what's it called?

what's it used for?

where does it grow?

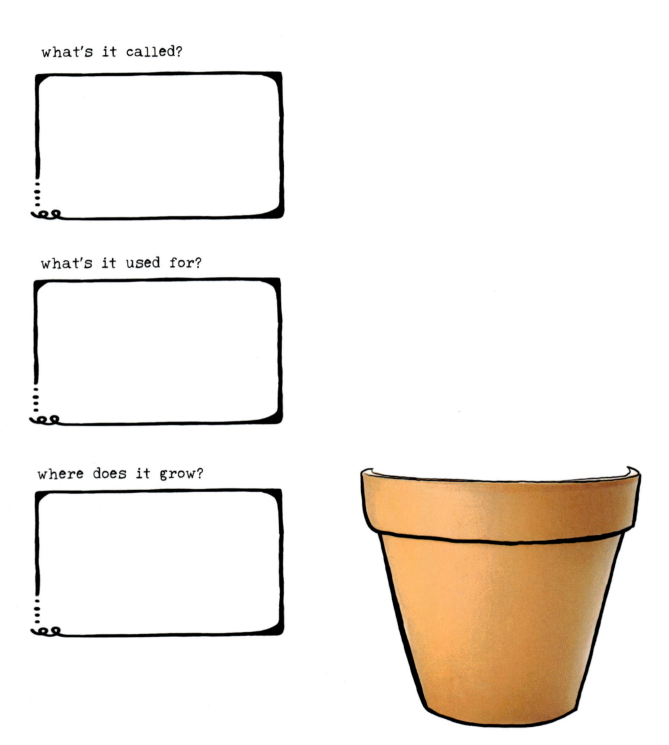

Connect the stars in any order. Create a constellation if you can.

A constellation is a group of stars connected together to make imaginary shapes in the night sky. They are usually named after mythological characters and are linked to numerous stories.

Made in United States
Orlando, FL
21 March 2023

31293436R00027